W9-BBO-290

Regina Public Library
BOOK SALE ITEM
Non-returnable

CANADIAN HISTORY TIMELINES

Confederation

Blaine Wiseman

Weigl

Published by Weigl Educational Publishers Limited
6325 – 10 Street SE
Calgary, Alberta, Canada
T2H 2Z9

Website: www.weigl.ca

Copyright © 2014 WEIGL EDUCATIONAL PUBLISHERS LIMITED
All rights reserved. No part of this publication may be reproduced, stored
in a retrieval system, or transmitted in any form or by any means, electronic,
mechanical, photocopying, recording, or otherwise, without the prior written
permission of the publisher.

Library and Archives Canada Cataloguing in Publication data available upon request.
ISBN 978-1-77071-274-4 (hardcover)
ISBN 978-1-77071-275-1 (softcover)
ISBN 978-1-77071-276-8 (multi-user eBook)

Printed in the United States of America in North Mankato, Minnesota
1 2 3 4 5 6 7 8 9 0 17 16 15 14 13

072013
WEP130613

We acknowledge the financial support of the Government of Canada through
the Canada Book Fund for our publishing activities.

Photograph and Text Credits
Library and Archives Canada: 6, 8, 9, 11, 13, 15, 17, 18–19, 21, 22–23, 25, 27
Getty Images: 4–5, 7, 26–27
Dreamstime: 29

Every reasonable effort has been made to trace ownership and to obtain
permission to reprint copyright material. The publishers would be pleased
to have any errors or omissions brought to their attention so that they may
be corrected in subsequent printings.

Editor
Pamela Dell

Project Coordinator
Aaron Carr

Designer
Terry Paulhus

All of the Internet URLs given in
the book were valid at the time of
publication. However, due to the
dynamic nature of the Internet,
some addresses may have changed,
or sites may have ceased to exist
since publication. While the
author and publisher regret any
inconvenience this may cause
readers, no responsibility for any
such changes can be accepted by
either the author or the publisher.

CONTENTS

The Confederates

Queen Victoria was the **monarch** of the British **Empire** leading up to **Confederation**. As part of the empire, Canada needed the queen's permission to become its own nation. The queen was strongly in favour of Confederation and happily granted it. She is sometimes called the Mother of Confederation. However, it was not the Queen alone who made Canada its own nation. Many people worked to make Canada an independent nation.

JOHN A. MACDONALD

John A. Macdonald was born in Scotland, but he moved to Canada with his family at the age of five. He was the leader of the Confederation movement and later became Canada's first prime minister.

GEORGE BROWN

George Brown was the leader of the Canadian Reform Party. Although he was the main rival of John A. Macdonald, another political leader, the two later joined together to achieve Confederation.

GEORGE-ÉTIENNE CARTIER

George-Étienne Cartier was another politician who worked with Macdonald and Brown to unite Canada. He helped ensure Quebec was part of Confederation.

Many important people helped Canada achieve Confederation, including 32 of Canada's most important leaders.

Queen Victoria ruled for more than 63 years. She is the longest serving monarch in British history.

C anada is a nation born of the struggles between other countries over hundreds of years. The nation's history is a story of rivalries, wars, and rebellions. The players in this story include **First Nations**, the **Métis**, Great Britain, France, and even the United States. All fought for control of the land that later became Canada.

During the early 1700s, France held most of the power in North America. The land it controlled was called New France. Great Britain's territory in North America was smaller. In 1756, the Seven Years' War broke out in Europe between France, Great Britain, and several other countries. This global conflict even reached across the Atlantic Ocean.

Canada was an important battleground in this war. On September 13, 1759, the British army defeated the French at the battle of the Plains of Abraham near Quebec City. As a result, New France became a British **colony**. Most of North America was now under the control of the British Empire.

Then, in 1775, the American Revolutionary War broke out. This war resulted in the birth of the United States of America. During the war, 50,000 Americans who were loyal to Great Britain left the United States and moved to Canada. The First Nations, the Métis, the French, the British, and these Americans who came to Canada would each play major roles in turning Canada into its own country. They would be among the key players in building the Canadian Confederation.

By the time Europeans arrived in North America, First Nations people had already lived there for thousands of years.

During the Seven Years' War, most First Nations fought on the side of the French.

Divided and United

Some French Canadians felt their language and culture were threatened by the English-speaking population. The British **Crown** tried to fix some of these concerns by creating the Constitutional Act. The act came into effect on December 26, 1791. This act divided Great Britain's new Canadian colony into two parts, called Upper Canada and Lower Canada. Upper Canada, what is now the province of Ontario, had the same laws as the British Empire. Lower Canada, which later became the province of Quebec, followed French law.

After the American Civil War, the British government wanted to remain in control of Canada. The British were worried that the new United States would try to take over Canada. They were right to be worried. In the summer of 1812, the United States went to war against the British Empire. English and French Canadians had fought against each other many times. Now they joined together to fight against the United States.

The Americans thought Canada would be an easy target. They were wrong. On December 24, 1814, after more than two years of fighting in both Canada and the United States, the two sides signed a peace **treaty**, called the Treaty of Ghent. The Canadians, both English and French, had defended their land against the Americans. This helped create a sense of **nationalism** among the peoples of Canada.

In 1814, during the War of 1812, British troops attacked Washington, D.C. They almost completely burned down the White House, the home of the president of the United States.

During the War of 1812, Britain pressed the attack against the Americans, attacking as far south as New Orleans, Louisiana.

Rebellions

As Canada grew, different groups of people developed different viewpoints. Most of the power belonged to British politicians, but the Canadian people wanted more control. They wanted to have a strong say in how they were governed. In 1837, the people began to rebel.

In the 1830s in Lower Canada, many workers and **habitants** were struggling to find food and work. Led by lawyer and politician Louis-Joseph Papineau, a group called the Patriotes demanded change. The British government tried to tighten its grip on Lower Canada, but the Patriotes resisted. From 1837 to 1838, the Patriotes mounted two rebellions. Both rebellions failed. More than 300 people, most of them rebels, were killed in battle. In the end, 58 Patriotes were **exiled** to Australia and 12 were convicted of **treason** and hanged.

Upper Canada saw similar struggles during these years. Americans who had settled in Canada before the War of 1812 were frustrated. They felt that the British government favoured the British citizens of Canada. In early December 1837, a man named William Lyon Mackenzie began planning a rebellion at Montgomery's Tavern in Toronto, along with about 1,000 rebels. Mackenzie thought they could take over the government of Upper Canada.

Just as the rebellion in Lower Canada had failed, so did Mackenzie's efforts. By the end of 1838, Mackenzie and his rebels had been defeated by a force of British **militia** and sympathetic volunteers. However, this was not the end. The Canadian people wanted control of their own country, and they were beginning to stand up for themselves.

In 1834, William Lyon Mackenzie became the first mayor of Toronto, Ontario.

Louis-Joseph Papineau was exiled for his role in the rebellions, but was allowed to return to Canada in 1845.

Coming Together

After the rebellions of 1837, Great Britain wanted to maintain even greater control over its rebellious Canadian colonies, but it also needed to lessen the conflicts between them. In 1840, the British **Parliament** presented a solution.

Called the Act of Union, it united the two provinces into one. Lower Canada was renamed Canada East and Upper Canada became Canada West. Together, as the Province of Canada, both regions were now represented by a single governmental body. The Act of Union also made English the official language of the parliament in Canada.

The Act of Union made it clear to Canadians that Canada East and Canada West needed to work together if they were ever to live in a united Canada independent of British rule. Heading up this movement for a so-called **responsible government** were leading politicians Robert Baldwin of Canada West and Louis LaFontaine of Canada East.

Their cause gained popularity quickly, and from 1848 and 1851, their leadership in parliament became known as the "Great Ministry." It was Canada's first form of responsible government, but it was only a beginning. The goal of Canadian Confederation was a long way off. Over the next 20 years, Canadians would see great changes in their pursuit of this goal.

Louis LaFontaine was so smart that his nickname in college was "The Big Brain."

Robert Baldwin was trained as a lawyer. He also helped create the University of Toronto from old King's College in 1849.

1864   1866–1867   1867   1869–1870   1871–1885   1885–TODAY

A Grand Coalition

By the 1860s, the Province of Canada was failing. The whole **economy** was struggling, and the government was in major conflict. Important decisions were being delayed. The different political parties were blocking each other from making any changes. The unity of the two Canadas seemed an impossible task.

In 1861, the American Civil War broke out. Once again, many worried that the United States would invade Canada. Canada's leaders realized that, to withstand the conflicts and changes, a unified leadership was more important than ever.

George Brown was the leader of the reform movement and a rival of John A. Macdonald. Despite the rivalry, Brown asked Macdonald's Conservatives and George-Étienne Cartier's Parti Bleu to work with him to improve the Canadian political system. For once, all of the parties stood together. They agreed that the best way to protect Canada from the Americans and to boost the economy was to bring the colonies of British North America together through Confederation.

On June 22, 1864, the three parties joined forces in the Canadian parliament. Their union, known as the Great Coalition, was a major step toward Confederation. The dream of **nationhood** for Canada was growing stronger.

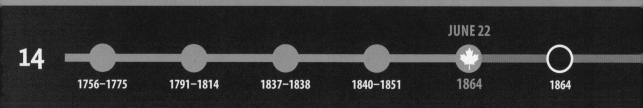

JUNE 22

1756–1775   1791–1814   1837–1838   1840–1851   1864   1864

"Let us be English or let us be French...but above all let us be Canadians!" John A. Macdonald

George Brown strongly believed that the views of French Canadians had to be taken into account for Canada to be united.

Meet Me in Charlottetown

With the Great Coalition in place, Canada had the opportunity to move more quickly toward Confederation. Both Canada West and Canada East were ready, but they wanted the other British North American colonies to join them as well.

The **maritime** colonies of Nova Scotia and New Brunswick had also showed an interest in Confederation. Their governments considered organizing a conference to discuss the matter, but they made little real effort until they got word that the Province of Canada had a strong interest in attending. With this news, and wanting Prince Edward Island (PEI) to agree to join in the discussions, Nova Scotia's governor set the conference for Charlottetown, PEI.

On September 1, 1864, representatives from the Province of Canada, including John A. Macdonald, George Brown, and George-Étienne Cartier, met with **delegates** from Nova Scotia, New Brunswick, and PEI. However, Newfoundland had not responded to the news in time to organize a delegation to attend. When the meetings ended eight days later on September 9, all delegates agreed that the matter was important enough for further discussion.

"I don't care for office for the sake of money, but for the sake of power, and for the sake of carrying out my own views of what is best for the country." John A. Macdonald

It took several meetings for the leaders to come to an agreement about Canada becoming its own country.

See You in Quebec

With all the Charlottetown attendees in agreement, a second conference was scheduled to continue working toward Confederation. On October 10, 1864, 33 delegates from various parts of British North America came together in Quebec City.

The purpose of the second conference was to hammer out the terms of Confederation. The discussions in Quebec, however, did not go as easily as those in Charlottetown. Experienced in constitutional law, John A. Macdonald had a major role in drafting the conference agreement, and he believed in a strong central government. He thought it was dangerous to give a great deal of power to the individual colonies and the Canadas, although many others disagreed.

By October 27, the 33 delegates had agreed on 72 resolutions, or decisions. Macdonald himself wrote 50 of them. These so-called Quebec Resolutions would go on to form the basis of the Canadian Confederation. The next step was to present their case to the British Parliament, which was still in control of the colonies.

On October 27, after the Quebec Resolutions were approved, an excited George Brown wrote to his wife: "We have the power in our hands (if it passes), to change it as we like. Hurrah!"

The Constitutional Act of 1791 divided Canada into Upper and Lower. By giving Upper Canada a constitution, it had set the path towards the Confederation talks almost 100 years later.

Off to London

On December 4, 1866, a small group of delegates from Canada, Nova Scotia, and New Brunswick met in London, England. The purpose of the London Conference was to review and polish the language of the Quebec Resolutions and then present them to the British government. Without the government's agreement, there would be no independent Canada.

In this polished document, known as the London Resolutions, the delegates set forth their case for Confederation. They then used the document to draft a bill called the British North America Act, which they presented to Britain's Queen Victoria.

On March 29, 1867, Queen Victoria signed the British North America Act. The delegates from New Brunswick, Nova Scotia, and the Province of Canada sailed home to prepare for becoming one nation. Newfoundland, Prince Edward Island, and other colonies would not join Confederation until later.

1756–1775   1791–1814   1837–1838   1840–1851   1864   1864

On February 16, 1867, during the London Conference, John A. Macdonald married his second wife, Agnes Bernard.

UPPER CANADA

The leaders who helped Canada become its own country are known as the Fathers of Confederation.

1864

1866–1867

1867

1869–1870

1871–1885

1885–TODAY

21

A New Nation

The "Fathers of Confederation" now had to decide who would be in charge of their newly created Canadian government. The decision was not difficult. John A. Macdonald, part of the Great Coalition and leader of the Confederation movement, became Canada's first prime minister. He was also knighted by Queen Victoria, becoming Sir John A. Macdonald.

Alexander Tilloch Galt became the first **federal** minister of finance, while George-Étienne Cartier was named the federal government's first minister of defence. George Brown, an original member of the Great Coalition along with Macdonald and Cartier, had helped draft the Quebec Resolutions. However, he had no hand in the completion of the Confederation. Brown had resigned from government office in 1865 because of conflicts with Macdonald and other politicians.

On July 1, 1867, the Dominion of Canada was officially born. In noisy celebrations across the land, with cannon fire and fireworks, Canadians celebrated the birth of their new nation.

LEGEND
- Dominion of Canada
- Rupert's Land
- United States
- British Colonies and unclaimed land

1756–1775   1791–1814   1837–1838   1840–1851   1864   1864

In 1867, the Canadian government started to think about building a railway to hold its claim on western North America.

Dominion of Canada, 1867

Hudson Bay

Atlantic Ocean

The Land Between

Canada was finally a nation, but it was still made up of only four provinces. There was work to be done in order to unite the entire country from the Atlantic Ocean to the Pacific Ocean.

One piece of territory the Canadians wanted was Rupert's Land, a vast area encircling Hudson Bay in the northwest. As part of British North America Act, Great Britain agreed to purchase Rupert's Land and give it to Canada. The official transfer was to take place on December 1, 1869, but other peoples considered the land theirs. Métis and First Nations people had lived on Rupert's Land for generations and did not want to give it up.

In October 1869, a Canadian official came to survey the land around the Red River Métis settlement. A Métis leader named Louis Riel mounted a protest. This conflict came to be known as the Red River Rebellion.

Over the winter, as the rebellion continued, Riel formed a government in what would later become Manitoba. In 1870, Rupert's Land was transferred to Canada. That same year, Manitoba and the Northwest Territory, both once part of Rupert's Land, became Canada's fifth and sixth provinces.

"In a little while it will be over. We may fail, but the rights for which we contend will not die." Louis Riel

In 1885, Louis Riel was put on trial for his role in a later rebellion called the North-West Resistance. He was sentenced to death and hanged. Today, Riel is considered a hero in many parts of Canada.

From Sea to Sea

On July 20, 1871, British Columbia joined the Confederation. Canada now included more than half the land in North America. The country stretched more than 5,000 kilometres from the Atlantic to the Pacific Ocean. However, connecting the nation from end to end would be a difficult task.

One of the terms agreed upon when British Columbia joined the Confederation was that the government would build a trade route linking the province with Ontario and Quebec. British Columbia wanted a wagon road, but Prime Minister Macdonald had bigger plans. Instead of a road, he envisioned a railway extending across the continent.

Construction on the Canadian Pacific Railway began in 1881. The work did not go smoothly. Hundreds of workers died laying tracks through forests, over rivers and lakes, and across the Rocky Mountains. There were many delays and setbacks.

On November 7, 1885, the last spike was driven into the track at Craigellachie, British Columbia. The Canadian Pacific Railway was finished. Canada had built the longest railway in the world.

The Canadian Pacific Railway company built many large train stations all over Canada, including in the new province of British Columbia. The railway truly had joined Canada.

The last spike was removed shortly after it was hammered in place. This was done to save it from being stolen by souvenir hunters. Another spike was then put in its place.

Just the Beginning

With the Canadian Pacific Railway complete in 1885, travel and transportation within Canada became much easier. Through the efforts of thousands of people, the country was truly united. In the following years, millions of people settled throughout Canada. During the 1900s, more provinces and territories joined the Confederation. Today, Canada includes 10 provinces and three territories.

From a country divided by politics and geography, a group of people built a powerful nation. Its history is one of struggles and triumphs and ongoing progress. Today, Canada is one of the most multicultural nations in the world. With the diversity of its people and its rich mix of cultures, Canada is a nation that its citizens are proud to call home.

"Whatever you do, adhere to the Union. We are a great country and shall become one of the greatest in the universe if we preserve it; we shall sink into insignificance and adversity if we suffer it to be broken." John A. Macdonald

1756–1775   1791–1814   1837–1838   1840–1851   1864   1864

Every July 1, on Canada Day, Canadians celebrate the vision and achievements of the Fathers of Confederation.

Brain Teaser

1. Who began planning a rebellion in December 1837?

2. Who was the British monarch during Canadian Confederation?

3. What three leaders formed the Great Coalition?

4. How many resolutions came out of the Quebec Conference in 1864?

5. On what date did Canada become a nation?

6. Who became the first prime minister of the new Canada?

7. What was built between 1881 and 1885 to connect Canada from coast to coast?

ANSWERS

1. William Lyon Mackenzie
2. Queen Victoria
3. John A. Macdonald, George Brown, and George-Étienne Cartier.
4. 72
5. July 1, 1867
6. John A. Macdonald
7. Canadian Pacific Railway

Further Information

Watch this video to learn more about Robert Baldwin and Louis LaFontaine **www.historica-dominion.ca/content/ heritage-minutes/baldwin-lafontaine**

Look at this timeline to learn more about Confederation **www. canadiangeographic.ca/atlas/themes. aspx?id=building&sub=building_basics_ confederation**

Find out more about Canadian Confederation here **www. collectionscanada.gc.ca/ confederation/kids/index-e.html**

Watch this video about responsible government **www.historica-dominion.ca/ content/heritage-minutes/ responsible-government?media_ type=41&media_category=27**

Read all about Sir John A. Macdonald at **www.collectionscanada.gc.ca/2/9/ h9-3030-e.html**

Read more about Confederation and Canadian history at this website **www.canadahistoryproject.ca/1867/ index.html**

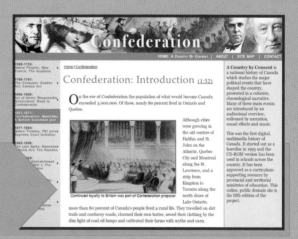

Glossary

colony: a foreign land settled by the people of a nation

Confederation: the joining of several British colonies into the country of Canada

Crown: the reigning monarch of country; represents the government of a country

delegates: people who act as representatives for other people or groups

economy: the money and business of a nation

empire: a group of countries and colonies under the rule of a single nation

exiled: forced to leave one's country

federal: the level of government that runs the country

First Nations: Aboriginal peoples of Canada, aside from Inuit and Métis

habitants: in Canada, people who rented land from wealthy landlords

maritime: areas near the ocean, such as Nova Scotia, New Brunswick, and Prince Edward Island

Métis: a nation of people that began when French and First Nations people had children together

militia: a group of regular citizens who volunteer to fight as soldiers

monarch: the queen or king of a country

nationalism: a feeling of pride for one's own nation

nationhood: the idea of being an independent nation

parliament: the highest law-making government body

responsible government: a government that operates according to the will of its people

treason: betrayal of one's country

treaty: a written agreement

Index